# The Best Facts For Smart Kids

# To Make You Think, Laugh, And Learn

*Outsmart Your Friends With Fascinating Facts About History, Science, Holidays, And More*

By David W. Leon

Written by David W. Leon
Illustrated by Rhiannon Perrin

# Table of Contents

Introduction ............7

Level 1: Discover Something New Today ............9

Level 2: Dazzle With Your Brainpower ............51

Level 3: Seize The Day And Broaden Your Horizons ........95

Level 4: Who In Your Family Is The Brainiest............136

Level 5: Discover The Unknown............178

Thank You & Leave A Review ............220

Your Free Gift ............222

Check Out The Full Series............224

# Introduction

I grew up absorbed in fact books, I loved watching Jeopardy in the afternoons, and I signed up for way too many email subscriptions just to get their daily trivia email blasts. One thing I noticed with fact books lately is that the newer books seem to be falling flat, and upon further research, it seems I'm not the only person who has seen this unfortunate shift.

- Instead of being easy to read, now most fact books are overwhelmingly text intensive with minimal or no visuals.
- Instead of providing unique or obscure facts, now most trivia books regurgitate the same information.
- Instead of being age appropriate, now some fact books swing widely from appropriate facts to unexpectedly dark facts.

I've decided to try my hand at solving the above issues and created a new way to engage with the trivia!

If you're like me and love to have fun while learning about crazy and quirky facts, then I might just have the solution for you. I hope you enjoy!

# Level 1
## Discover Something New Today

## Questions 1-20

Some Things You'll Know And Some Things You'll Learn!

Be Sure To Share What You've Learned With Others!

# The Best Facts
# For Smart Kids

## Question 1

In China, "The Spring Festival" is also commonly referred to as?

a)  Qingming Festival

b)  Hungry Ghost Festival

c)  Chinese New Year

d)  Double Seventh Day

# David W. Leon
# Fun Facts Books

**Answer 1**

Celebrated for thousands of years, the fifteen-day annual festival is known as both the Spring Festival and the Chinese New Year. To celebrate, there are firecrackers, and red is present everywhere, from the money given to people in red envelopes to the red decorations and lanterns adorning people's homes. Luck is a very important part of the Chinese New Year, with families sweeping and cleaning their homes before the holiday to get rid of any lingering bad luck from the previous year.

# The Best Facts
# For Smart Kids

## Question 2

The Leaning Tower of Pisa is in what country?

a)  Italy

b)  Greece

c)  Spain

d)  Egypt

**Answer 2**

Built to serve as a church's bell tower, the Leaning Tower of Pisa is one of Italy's most popular tourist sites. It was not built to lean but began leaning during its construction during the Middle Ages. The tower was constructed on soft ground and the weight of the taller floors caused the building to slightly sink.

# The Best Facts
# For Smart Kids

**Question 3**

From which organ did the philosopher Aristotle believe emotions came from?

a) Brain

b) Heart

c) Spleen

d) Tongue

**Answer 3**

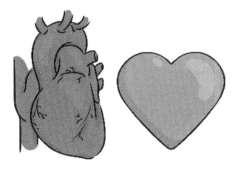

Aristotle viewed the heart as the primary organ responsible for various psychological and physiological functions, including emotions, perception, cognition, and sensory integration. He believed that emotions were directly connected to the heart's activity and that different emotional states could be attributed to specific movements and conditions of the heart.

# The Best Facts
# For Smart Kids

**Question 4**

While he made several great inventions, Benjamin Franklin is well known for which remarkable experiment?

a)  The radio

b)  The lightning rod

c)  The telephone

d)  X-rays

# David W. Leon
# Fun Facts Books

**Answer 4**

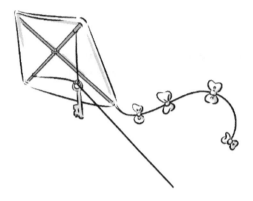

Benjamin Franklin had a prolific life as a politician and an inventor. Franklin conducted an experiment with a kite and a key to test electricity, which led him to invent the lightning rod. He also invented the rocking chair and bifocal glasses.

# The Best Facts
# For Smart Kids

## Question 5

What festival is held at the end of the Chinese New Year, on the fifteenth day of the first month of the Chinese lunar calendar?

a) The Double Ninth Festival

b) Winter Solstice

c) Laba Festival

d) Lantern Festival

**Answer 5**

Marking the first full moon of the new year, the Lantern Festival includes celebrations with brightly colored lanterns, dragon dances, and fireworks. The Lantern Festival celebrates a time of forgiveness and reconciliation.

# The Best Facts
# For Smart Kids

## Question 6

What country is part of Niagara Falls located in?

a) Iceland

b) Russia

c) Mexico

d) Canada

# David W. Leon
# Fun Facts Books

**Answer 6**

Located between Lake Erie and Lake Ontario, Niagara Falls is shared by the United States and Canada. The city of Ontario overlooks the Horseshoe Falls, also called the Canadian Falls. Melting glaciers formed Niagara Falls over 12,000 years ago and the water generates enough electricity for the nearby city of Ontario.

# The Best Facts
# For Smart Kids

**Question 7**

What do some animals, such as bears, do in winter when food becomes scarce?

a) Hibernate

b) Migrate

c) Huddle

d) Burrow

# David W. Leon
# Fun Facts Books

**Answer 7**

Bears and other animals hibernate as a survival strategy to cope with harsh environmental conditions, particularly during cold winters when food becomes scarce. Hibernation patterns can vary among species, with some animals entering deep hibernation and others engaging in torpor, which is more of a light sleep state.

# The Best Facts
# For Smart Kids

**Question 8**

In 1844, the telegraph was invented as the first form of electrical communication. This allowed for quicker communication than regular mail. What was the next major advancement in long-distance communication?

a) Radio

b) Telephone

c) Television

d) Texting

**Answer 8**

Although Alexander Graham Bell is credited with inventing the telephone in 1876, it had been already invented in 1849 by Antonio Meucci (Library of Congress, 2022). On another hand, the radio was invented by Guglielmo Marconi in 1895, in Italy. Therefore, regardless of the first person to have the idea, the telephone came before the radio.

# The Best Facts
# For Smart Kids

**Question 9**

During what Chinese festival do family members visit and clean the graves of their ancestors?

a) Qingming Festival

b) Yuan Xiao Festival

c) Qixi Festival

d) Cold Food Festival

**Answer 9**

Also known as "Tomb Sweeping Day," the Qingming Festival is a time when families visit their ancestor's graves to clean them, burn incense, and offer the spirits wine and tea. In addition to honoring their departed loved ones, families decorate their doors and gates with willow branches to ward off bad luck.

# The Best Facts
# For Smart Kids

**Question 10**

Sitting in Port Jackson, in what country is the Sydney Opera House located?

a) Fiji

b) Australia

c) Japan

d) New Zealand

# David W. Leon
# Fun Facts Books

**Answer 10**

Designed by Danish architect Jørn Utzon after winning a contest, the sail-shaped Sydney Opera House is in Sydney, Australia. There are 2,679 seats in the concert hall and 1,500 seats in the ballet theater. There are also restaurants and a recording studio on-site.

# The Best Facts
# For Smart Kids

## Question 11

What is the common cold?

a)  A type of virus

b)  A type of bacteria

c)  A type of allergy

d)  A type of cell

**Answer 11**

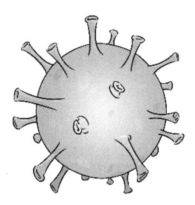

Because the common cold is a type of virus, antibiotics and over-the-counter medications do not cure a cold. Over 200 viruses can cause a cold, which is why it's important to wipe down surfaces and wash your hands frequently.

# The Best Facts
# For Smart Kids

**Question 12**

Who invented the telescope?

a)  Benjamin Franklin

b)  Isaac Newton

c)  Stephen Hawking

d)  Galileo Galilei

**Answer 12**

The Italian scientist Galileo Galilei created the first telescope to look at the night sky and see how planets and stars moved. He made an amazing contribution to understanding the universe.

# The Best Facts
# For Smart Kids

**Question 13**

What Chinese festival is held to celebrate Qu Yuan, a famous Chinese poet?

a) Shanghai Festival

b) Dragon Boat Festival

c) Duanwu Festival

d) Mid-Autumn Festival

**Answer 13**

Now considered a national hero, Qu Yuan's death is honored with the Dragon Boat Festival each year. However, some scholars believe that the festival originated from the fifth lunar month of the Chinese year being named the "month of poison"; because that's when poisonous creatures like snakes, scorpions, and spiders emerge. Whatever its origins, the festival is marked by participating in, or watching, dragon boat races.

# The Best Facts
# For Smart Kids

**Question 14**

Angkor Watt is an iconic Hindu temple located in what country?

a) Vietnam

b) Cambodia

c) China

d) India

**Answer 14**

Covered in intricate carvings and motifs, including nymphs with thirty-seven different hairstyles, this temple is in Cambodia. It is the largest religious building in the world and was built with sandstone blocks.

# The Best Facts
# For Smart Kids

## Question 15

Which animal has the highest blood pressure?

a) Wolves

b) Bears

c) Elephants

d) Giraffes

# David W. Leon
# Fun Facts Books

**Answer 15**

Because their necks are so long, giraffes have sky-high blood pressure. The high blood pressure in giraffes allows for efficient blood circulation throughout their long necks and bodies. It is an adaptation that enables giraffes to thrive in their habitats, where they need to reach the leaves of tall trees for food and maintain blood flow to their brains even when they lower their heads to drink water.

# The Best Facts
# For Smart Kids

**Question 16**

When was writing invented?

a) During the Renaissance

b) Around five thousand years ago

c) During the Middle Ages

d) After the invention of the printing press

# David W. Leon
# Fun Facts Books

**Answer 16**

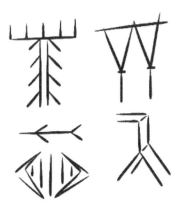

Writing was invented in Asian Mesopotamia about five thousand years ago. The Sumerians, people who lived in modern-day Iraq, were the first to turn the sound of spoken languages into characters. They wrote Sumerian and also foreign languages.

# The Best Facts
# For Smart Kids

**Question 17**

In which year was Father's Day made an official United States' holiday?

a) 1910

b) 1972

c) 1945

d) 1956

43

**Answer 17**

Father's Day was first celebrated in Washington state on June 19, 1910, but it did not become an official holiday recognized by all states until 1972. A Spokane, Washington, native is credited with the creation of Father's Day. She was one of six children raised by her father after her mother died and felt that fathers should have a holiday like Mother's Day.

# The Best Facts
# For Smart Kids

**Question 18**

In what European country is the Brandenburg Gate located?

a) Poland

b) Portugal

c) Belarus

d) Germany

# David W. Leon
# Fun Facts Books

**Answer 18**

Commissioned by King Frederick William II, the Brandenburg Gate was constructed between 1788 and 1791 in Germany. When the city of Berlin was divided during the Cold War, the gate became a symbol of freedom and unity. Because of the location of the Berlin Wall, neither East nor West Berliners could visit the Brandenburg Gate. After being restored in 2002, the gate has become a popular tourist attraction.

# The Best Facts
# For Smart Kids

**Question 19**

What is biological psychology?

a) The study of the links between the brain and psychology

b) The study of the psychology of organisms

c) Investigating the influence of biological factors on behavior

d) The study of aging and the mind

**Answer 19**

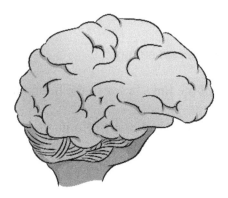

Biological psychology is a branch of psychology that investigates how biological factors influence human behavior and mental processes. It examines the interplay between the brain, genetics, hormones, and other physiological processes to understand psychological phenomena.

**Question 20**

Leonardo Da Vinci, Michelangelo Buonarotti, and Sandro Botticelli are some of the most relevant figures of which artistic movement of the Modern Era?

a) Romanticism

b) Enlightenment

c) Renaissance

d) Impressionism

**Answer 20**

They are all painters from the Renaissance. This artistic movement took place in Europe between the 15th and 17th centuries. It is a bridge between the Middle Ages and the Modern Era. Artists rediscovered and brought back the legacy of ancient Greek and Roman culture.

# Level 2
## Dazzle With Your Brainpower

### Questions 21-40

Did You Get All Those Right?

Maybe I Can Stump You With These Next Questions!

# The Best Facts
# For Smart Kids

**Question 21**

What annual holiday in the United States is celebrated on the second Sunday in May?

a)  Easter

b)  Mother's Day

c)  Memorial Day

d)  Labor Day

# David W. Leon
# Fun Facts Books

**Answer 21**

A Philadelphia woman named Ann Jarvis is credited with the creation of Mother's Day after she held a memorial service for her mother in May 1907. The holiday quickly caught on and President Woodrow Wilson made it an official US holiday in 1914.

# The Best Facts
# For Smart Kids

**Question 22**

George Washington, Thomas Jefferson, and Theodore Roosevelt all appear on Mount Rushmore; who is the fourth president you can see on this giant monument?

a)  Abraham Lincoln

b)  John F. Kennedy

c)  Jimmy Carter

d)  Andrew Jackson

**Answer 22**

Each president on Mount Rushmore has a special place in American history: Washington for being the first President, Jefferson for authoring the Declaration of Independence, and Theodore Roosevelt for his passionate conservation. Abraham Lincoln appears on the giant monument because he was the President during the Civil War and issued the emancipation proclamation declaring the end of slavery in the USA.

# The Best Facts
# For Smart Kids

**Question 23**

Why should you not fold your arms during a job interview?

a)  It startles the interviewer

b)  It can be perceived as a defensive gesture

c)  It suggests that you know more than the interviewer

d)  It suggests you're not taking the interview seriously

**Answer 23**

Body language plays a crucial role in communication. Folding your arms across your chest can be interpreted as a defensive or guarded posture, signaling a lack of openness or receptiveness to the interviewer's questions or ideas.

# The Best Facts
# For Smart Kids

**Question 24**

Which French ruler, known as a great military strategist and politician, was able to expand the French Empire in 1799?

a) Julius Caesar

b) Napoleon Bonaparte

c) Cardinal Richelieu

d) Philip the Handsome

**Answer 24**

Napoleon Bonaparte was born on the island of Corsica, France. When the French Revolution happened, he was a general in the army. In 1799, he led a coup d'état and became emperor of France. The limits of his empire reached the frozen lands of the Russian steppe.

# The Best Facts
# For Smart Kids

**Question 25**

What ancient Roman holiday honors the god of seed and the promise of good harvest?

a) Neptunalia

b) Agonalia

c) Parilia

d) Saturnalia

**Answer 25**

Initially celebrated during the winter solstice and then evolving into a week-long celebration, Saturnalia was a time when social norms were relaxed in Ancient Rome. The festival was marked by banquets, wine, singing, and games. Elements of this Roman holiday went on to be included in the December holidays of Christmas and New Year.

# The Best Facts
# For Smart Kids

**Question 26**

William F. Baker, a Chicago architect, designed the world's tallest building, which is?

a) Taipei 101

b) Sear Tower

c) Empire State Building

d) Burj Khalifa

# David W. Leon
# Fun Facts Books

**Answer 26**

With 163 floors and towering approximately 2,717 feet (828 meters), the Burj Khalifa in Dubai, United Arab Emirates, is the tallest building in the world. Designed by William Baker, an architect with a Chicago firm, the skyscraper opened in 2010, although construction wasn't fully completed when the building opened. The Burj Khalifa also holds the record for the world's tallest freestanding structure, the world's highest occupied floor, and the world's highest outdoor observation deck.

# The Best Facts
# For Smart Kids

**Question 27**

What living thing can absorb carbon dioxide and mitigate climate change?

a) Cows

b) Trees

c) Cars

d) Rocks

**Answer 27**

By absorbing carbon dioxide and storing carbon, trees help to reduce the concentration of greenhouse gasses in the atmosphere. Trees absorb carbon dioxide through photosynthesis, a process in which Chlorophyll captures the energy from sunlight and uses this energy to convert carbon dioxide into glucose (a type of sugar) and oxygen. As a byproduct of photosynthesis, trees release oxygen back into the atmosphere, helping to fight climate change.

# The Best Facts
# For Smart Kids

**Question 28**

How long did the Hundred Years' War actually last?

a) Over a hundred years

b) Exactly a hundred years

c) A bit less than a hundred years

d) It lasted 20 years

# David W. Leon
# Fun Facts Books

**Answer 28**

The Hundred Years' War was fought between France and England, primarily regarding territory, over a span of 116 years. The war can be divided into four phases of major battles. It resulted in the French triumph and the English loss of territory in continental Europe.

# The Best Facts
# For Smart Kids

**Question 29**

What were holidays called in Ancient Rome?

a) Feriae

b) Gala

c) Fiesta

d) Advent

# David W. Leon
# Fun Facts Books

**Answer 29**

Usually observed by prayers, sacrifices, visits to temples, and feasts, the Romans called their public holidays Feriae. There were three types of Roman holidays: feriae stativae (holidays on held on the same day each year), feriae conceptivae (moveable feasts celebrated each year by priests and magistrates), and feriae imperativae (irregular holidays usually held after war victories and emergencies).

# The Best Facts
# For Smart Kids

## Question 30

What kind of grove is a popular tourist destination in Arashiyama district in Kyoto, Japan?

a) Cherry Blossom

b) Red Pine

c) Bamboo

d) Camphor

**Answer 30**

Covering roughly six miles (16 square kilometers), the Arashiyama Bamboo Grove is one of the most photographed places in the Kyoto district. The grove of massively tall bamboo trees is open twenty-four hours a day and is described as a dream-like experience. The Japanese Ministry of the Environment has recognized the rustling bamboo forest as one of the "100 Soundscapes of Japan."

# The Best Facts
# For Smart Kids

**Question 31**

A forensic entomologist would study what when examining a corpse?

a) Insects

b) Blood

c) Finger Bones

d) Glands

**Answer 31**

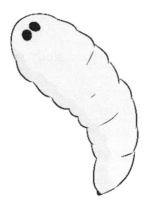

By examining the types of insects present, their developmental stages, and the environmental conditions, entomologists can estimate the postmortem interval (PMI) or the time that has passed since death. Their work often involves collecting insect specimens, conducting field investigations, analyzing data, and presenting their findings in court as expert witnesses.

# The Best Facts
# For Smart Kids

**Question 32**

Which of the following women was a French heroine in the Hundred Years' War?

a)  Joan of Arc

b)  Elizabeth from Castille

c)  Cleopatra

d)  Marie Antoinette

**Answer 32**

At 19 years old, Joan of Arc led the French army in one of the most important battles. She helped to lift the Siege of Orléans, which renewed the French people's morale to keep fighting and repel the English. She was later declared a martyr by the Catholic Church.

# The Best Facts
# For Smart Kids

**Question 33**

What is the name of the Roman holiday held at the end of March for the goddess Minerva?

a)  Floralia

b)  Vulcanalia

c)  Quinquatria

d)  Consualia

**Answer 33**

Minerva, the goddess of war and wisdom, was honored by ancient Romans in an annual spring festival held in March. Since Minerva is the goddess of the intellect, it was a time when educators were given gifts, and all were given a break from school. For five days, Romans celebrated Quinquatria by attending all kinds of art performances, including plays and dances.

# The Best Facts
# For Smart Kids

**Question 34**

The Little Mermaid statue in Copenhagen, Denmark, was inspired by the fairy tale written by?

a)  Hans Christian Anderson

b)  Jacob Grimm

c)  Lewis Carrol

d)  Frank Baum

**Answer 34**

Danish brewer Carl Jacobsen fell in love with The Little Mermaid after seeing a ballet performance based on the fairy tale by Hans Christian Anderson. Jacobsen asked the sculptor Edvard Eriksen to create the sculpture based on the likeness of Ellen Price, the dancer who played the mermaid in the ballet. This famous statue is located in Copenhagen Harbor.

# The Best Facts
# For Smart Kids

**Question 35**

What element is found in the Earth and is important for strong teeth and bones?

a) Calcium

b) Magnesium

c) Sodium

d) Titanium

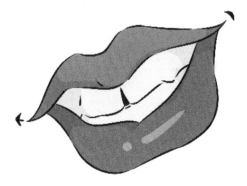

# David W. Leon
# Fun Facts Books

**Answer 35**

Calcium is an essential mineral that plays a crucial role in maintaining the health and strength of teeth and bones. It is a major component of hydroxyapatite, the mineralized matrix that gives strength and rigidity to bones and teeth. In the Earth's crust, calcium is one of the most abundant elements, commonly found in the form of calcium carbonate (limestone, chalk) and calcium silicates.

# The Best Facts
# For Smart Kids

**Question 36**

Who were the only people allowed to participate in tournaments and jousts in the Middle Ages?

a) Kings and princes

b) Peasants

c) Priests

d) Nobles

**Answer 36**

Tournaments and jousts were reserved for the nobles, the only ones who could be knights. Society was divided into strata during the Middle Ages, each of them with a role. Nobles had to protect the population. These competitions were opportunities to train their skills as soldiers.

# The Best Facts
# For Smart Kids

**Question 37**

What was the name of the Roman god of fire celebrated each year on August 23rd in Ancient Rome?

a) Vulcan

b) Jupiter

c) Ceres

d) Vesta

**Answer 37**

Hoping to appease the god of fire during the dry month of August, Vulcanalia was created to celebrate and appease Vulcan. The holiday was marked by sacrifices to the god in the hopes that he would spare their lives and crops from natural disasters. After the destruction of Pompeii, the number of sacrifices increased because people were afraid the volcano would erupt again.

# The Best Facts
# For Smart Kids

**Question 38**

What Seattle museum holds science fiction, horror movies, and video games exhibits?

a)  Seattle Art Museum

b)  National Nordic Museum

c)  Henry Art Gallery

d)  Museum of Pop Culture (MoPOP)

# David W. Leon
# Fun Facts Books

**Answer 38**

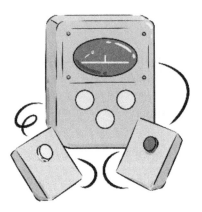

*Infinite Worlds of Science Fiction, Indie Game Revolution, and Scared to Death: The Thrill of Horror Film* are three permanent exhibits at the Museum of Pop Culture, also known as MoPOP. MoPOP encourages visitors to interact with their displays; they can play 20 video games from around the world and explore musical instruments in the many music exhibits.

# The Best Facts
# For Smart Kids

**Question 39**

What do camels store in their lumps?

a) Water

b) Fat

c) Food

d) Nothing

**Answer 39**

Camels do not store water in their humps as is commonly believed. Instead, their humps are reservoirs of fatty tissue. These fatty deposits serve as a source of energy when food and water are scarce.

# The Best Facts
# For Smart Kids

**Question 40**

What is the name of the city that, according to Homer, was conquered by the Greek army using a giant wooden horse?

a) Athens

b) Troy

c) Tebas

d) Rome

# David W. Leon
# Fun Facts Books

**Answer 40**

Legendary Troy was located on the eastern coast of modern-day Turkey. According to the Iliad, the Trojans found a huge wooden horse at the gates of the city. Greek soldiers were hidden inside and when the wooden horse was taken into the city, they came out and conquered Troy within a few hours.

You're almost halfway through!

If you've made it this far, I assume you are a true smartie who is willing to learn new things.

Remember, it is totally fine to not get every question right. This game is designed to stretch your mind and teach you new facts from around the world and throughout time!

If you have 2 minutes before the next level, providing feedback will greatly help me for writing future books and will also help other readers when looking at this book.

What do you think of the book so far?

Open the camera app on your phone
Hold phone so the QR Code appears in view
Tap the pop-up link for the QR Code

# Level 3
## Seize The Day
## And Broaden Your Horizons

## Questions 41-60

The World Is a Diverse Place!

I Hope You Discover Something New About Another Culture And Humankind's Robust History

# The Best Facts
# For Smart Kids

**Question 41**

What ancient Roman holiday was celebrated in April with flower garlands and wreaths?

a) Tubilustrium

b) Larentalia

c) Floralia

d) Vinalia

**Answer 41**

The spring festival of Floralia that began in Rome around 240 or 238 B.C. is an early example of a May Day celebration. The games and theatrical productions that marked this holiday were called Ludi Florales.

# The Best Facts
# For Smart Kids

**Question 42**

What artist painted over 300 figures for the Sistine Chapel in Rome, Italy?

a) Michelangelo

b) Botticelli

c) Raphael

d) Titian

# David W. Leon
# Fun Facts Books

**Answer 42**

Pope Julius II chose the painter Michelangelo Buonarroti to paint the ceiling of the Sistine Chapel. Initially, he was only supposed to paint the twelve apostles but painted several frescoes, including The Last Judgment and The Creation of Adam.

# The Best Facts
# For Smart Kids

**Question 43**

Which scientific technique is commonly used by archaeologists to determine the age of organic materials?

a) Carbon Dating

b) Radiography

c) Hieroglyphics

d) Spectroscopy

# David W. Leon
# Fun Facts Books

**Answer 43**

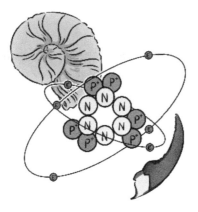

Carbon dating is a method used by scientists to determine the age of organic materials, such as ancient artifacts or fossils. It relies on the fact that all living things contain a small amount of a radioactive form of carbon called carbon-14.

# The Best Facts
# For Smart Kids

**Question 44**

In the Modern Era, commerce between America and Europe across the Atlantic Ocean was intense. Who did navigators and merchants fear running into on their trips across the sea?

a)  The British Royal Navy

b)  Corsairs and pirates

c)  Scientific explorers

d)  The native people

**Answer 44**

Navigators and merchants were afraid of being stormed by corsairs, who worked for the monarchs, and pirates, who were self-employed. After arriving in America, European ships traded for goods and metals taken from the colonies. Pirates and corsairs hunted the ships and stole from them.

# The Best Facts
# For Smart Kids

**Question 45**

What is the name of the horse-racing holiday in Ancient Rome?

a) Equirria

b) Lumeria

c) Augustalia

d) Bona Dea

**Answer 45**

Held in honor of Mars and instituted by Romulus, the festival of Equirria started on sundown of February 26th and ended with a sacrifice on the morning of February 27th. This holiday is also believed to be a time when the cavalry would rest.

# The Best Facts
# For Smart Kids

**Question 46**

What is the name of the abbey built during the Middle Ages in France between Normandy and Brittany?

a) Westminster Abbey

b) Mont-Saint-Michel

c) Saint-Denis

d) Bobbio Abbey

# David W. Leon
# Fun Facts Books

**Answer 46**

Dedicated to the archangel Michael, Mont-Saint-Michel is a Benedictine abbey famous for its Gothic architecture. The area's natural beauty and the abbey's impressive architecture are why Mont-Saint-Michel is known as "The Wonder of the West".

# The Best Facts
# For Smart Kids

## Question 47

How many muscles does a cat have in each ear?

a)  6

b)  15

c)  21

d)  32

**Answer 47**

Cats have about thirty-two muscles in each ear. These muscles allow them to move and control the position of their ears, which helps them detect sounds from different directions. Cats are known for their exceptional hearing, and their highly mobile ears play a significant role.

# The Best Facts
# For Smart Kids

**Question 48**

What did Marco Polo do?

a) He was a merchant and an explorer

b) He was a philosopher

c) He was a painter and a sculptor

d) He was a professor and a scientist

**Answer 48**

Marco Polo lived in Venice in the 1200s. At the time, European people didn't know much about the world beyond the Mediterranean Sea. Marco Polo traveled further and explored Asia. Once back in Europe, he told about his journeys and inspired other adventurers and explorers.

# The Best Facts
# For Smart Kids

**Question 49**

What German holiday features a procession of children holding lanterns?

a) Martinstag

b) Weihnachten

c) Oktoberfest

d) Vatertag

# David W. Leon
# Fun Facts Books

**Answer 49**

A holiday in honor of St. Martin, Martinstag usually features an evening procession by children carrying brightly lit lanterns. In some places, children go door-to-door and ask for candy and cookies.

# The Best Facts
# For Smart Kids

**Question 50**

What poet designed the Golden Gate Bridge and wrote the poem "A Mighty Task Is Done" at its completion?

a) Walt Whitman

b) Joseph Strauss

c) Robert Frost

d) Langston Hughes

# David W. Leon
# Fun Facts Books

**Answer 50**

In 1920, Joseph Strauss submitted plans for a symmetrical cantilever-suspension hybrid bridge design that both the public and the press found ugly. After meeting with a design team, Strauss eventually decided upon a conventional suspension bridge with Art Deco-style towers. When the bridge opened in 1937, Strauss read his poem as a tribute to the men who built the Golden Gate Bridge.

# The Best Facts
# For Smart Kids

**Question 51**

Why is the Earth getting warmer?

a) The planet is moving closer to the sun

b) A hole in the ozone layer

c) Greenhouse gasses in our atmosphere

d) The melting of glaciers

## Answer 51

Certain gasses in the Earth's atmosphere, known as greenhouse gasses, trap heat from the Sun and prevent it from escaping back into space. This natural process, called the greenhouse effect, is essential for supporting life on Earth, but human activities such as burning fossil fuels (coal, oil, and natural gas) have significantly increased the concentration of greenhouse gasses in the atmosphere. This enhanced greenhouse effect leads to more heat being trapped, causing the Earth's temperature to rise.

# The Best Facts
# For Smart Kids

**Question 52**

In which sea did pirates hunt and plunder the ships that left America towards Europe, carrying gold, silver, and goods, in the 17th and 18th centuries?

a)  The Mediterranean

b)  The Chinese

c)  The Aegean

d)  The Caribbean

# David W. Leon
## Fun Facts Books

**Answer 52**

During the 17th and 18th centuries, trading between the European powers and their American colonies was centered in the Atlantic Ocean. Most of the ships headed to ports on the shores of the Caribbean Sea in Central America, where pirates hunted their targets.

# The Best Facts
# For Smart Kids

**Question 53**

What German holiday features a drink called Feuerzangenbowle?

a) Ostern

b) May Day

c) Mariä Lichtmess

d) Neujahr

**Answer 53**

Composed of red wine, rum, oranges, lemons, cinnamon, and cloves, Feuerzangenbowle is a popular drink on Neujahr, the German word for New Year's. In addition to the Feuerzangenbowle, many Germans send cards or letters to loved ones at this time of the year.

# The Best Facts
# For Smart Kids

**Question 54**

If you travel to Rio de Janeiro for Carnaval, what kind of dance schools will be performed?

a) Samba

b) Tango

c) Cha-Cha

d) Bossa Nova

**Answer 54**

At Carnaval, Samba schools compete in the Sambodromo and are judged for their dancing, singing, costumes, and parade floats. Usually held in a stadium, the dancing and parade occurs in the middle while the audience watches from the side.

# The Best Facts
# For Smart Kids

**Question 55**

A popular food in Japan, which of these has killed diners with its powerful toxicity?

a) Octopus

b) Jellyfish

c) Puffer

d) Tuna

**Answer 55**

Certain species of pufferfish contain a potent neurotoxin called tetrodotoxin, which can be found in various parts of the fish, including the liver, ovaries, and skin. The toxin is extremely poisonous and can lead to paralysis, respiratory failure, and even death if consumed in sufficient quantities. In Japan, highly skilled and licensed chefs are trained to prepare puffer fish dishes, but even with these precautions, pufferfish poisonings have occurred due to improper preparation.

# The Best Facts
# For Smart Kids

## Question 56

Which country did Marie Antoinette rule?

a)  The United States

b)  The Russian Empire

c)  France

d)  Greece

**Answer 56**

Marie Antoinette married the French heir to the throne, Louis, who would later become Louis XVI. Therefore, Marie Antoinette became queen of France. They were the sovereigns when the French Revolution began. Both were condemned to death by a popular trial.

# The Best Facts
# For Smart Kids

**Question 57**

Which saint is credited with driving the snakes out of Ireland and with using the shamrock to explain the holy trinity to the Irish?

a) St. Michael

b) St. Patrick

c) St. Peter

d) Padre Pio

**Answer 57**

Celebrated both in Ireland and the United States on March 17th, St. Patrick is the patron saint of Ireland. Large St. Patrick's Day parades are held every year in New York City and Boston, two American cities with a large population of Irish immigrants.

# The Best Facts
# For Smart Kids

**Question 58**

What force of nature created the Giant's Causeway in Northern Ireland?

a)  Hurricane

b)  Tornado

c)  Volcanic Eruption

d)  Earthquake

**Answer 58**

After a volcanic eruption, layers of basalt formed on the chalky landscape, and lava filled the river valley, creating the Giant's Causeway. However, Irish legend states that a giant named Finn McCool created the causeway to fight a Scottish competitor.

# The Best Facts
# For Smart Kids

## Question 59

What is chalk made of?

a) Limestone

b) Chalk

c) Beryl

d) Agate

**Answer 59**

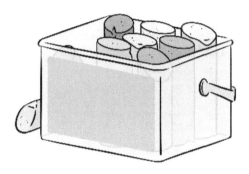

Chalk is primarily composed of limestone, a form of calcium carbonate; a soft, sedimentary rock formed by the accumulation of tiny marine organisms such as plankton and algae over millions of years. These organisms possess hard shells made of calcium carbonate, and when they die, their remains settle on the ocean floor. Over time, these remains are compacted and undergo geological processes to form chalk deposits.

# The Best Facts
# For Smart Kids

**Question 60**

Who were the first Europeans to arrive in Australia in the 17th century and give it the name of New Holland?

a) The Spanish

b) The Dutch

c) The Maoris

d) The Japanese

**Answer 60**

In the 17th century, European expeditions explored the African coasts and the islands in the Pacific Ocean, including Australia. The first to arrive on this huge island was the Dutch explorer Willem Janszoon. However, the Portuguese, Spanish, and Chinese also claimed to have been the first.

# Level 4
## Who In Your Family Is The Brainiest

## Questions 61-80

Have You Tried Testing Your Family Members With This Game?

See Who Can Get The Most Questions Right In This Next Level!

# The Best Facts
# For Smart Kids

**Question 61**

Which holiday in the United States prompted Taco Bell to falsely announce they had bought the Liberty Bell and renamed it "The Taco Liberty Bell?"

a) Cinco de Mayo

b) April Fool's Day

c) Truman Day

d) Father's Day

# David W. Leon
# Fun Facts Books

**Answer 61**

Once a two-day holiday in 18th-century England, April Fool's Day is now celebrated on April 1st in the United States. While the holiday's origins are a mystery, some historians believe it was influenced by the ancient Roman festival of "Hilaria," a joyful festival that occurred at the end of March.

# The Best Facts
# For Smart Kids

**Question 62**

Over what English palace is the Royal Standard flown only when the sovereign is in residence?

a)  Winter Palace

b)  Palace of Versailles

c)  Amber Palace

d)  Buckingham Palace

**Answer 62**

As the London residence of the British royals, Buckingham Palace only flies the royal flag when the monarch is in residence. Situated in the borough of Westminster, the palace features the King's art collection and impressive gardens. Queen Victoria was the first monarch to reside in Buckingham Palace.

# The Best Facts
# For Smart Kids

**Question 63**

Where were the oldest known cave paintings discovered, tentatively dated back 32,000 years?

a)  Egypt

b)  Iran

c)  France

d)  Germany

**Answer 63**

Chauvet Cave, located in southern France, is home to some of the oldest known cave paintings in the world. These paintings, dating back approximately 32,000 years, offer valuable insights into prehistoric human culture and artistic expression.

# The Best Facts
# For Smart Kids

**Question 64**

Which global empire declared Australia one of its colonies in the 1700s?

a)  England

b)  France

c)  The Russian Empire

d)  Netherlands

**Answer 64**

The first Dutch explorers didn't settle in Australia. Instead, the English took possession of the island in 1770 in the name of King George III. In the beginning, they didn't establish any trading relationships. They wanted the new lands to accommodate convicts from England.

# The Best Facts
# For Smart Kids

**Question 65**

In what year was the first Earth Day celebrated in the United States?

a)  1968

b)  1975

c)  1981

d)  1970

# David W. Leon
# Fun Facts Books

**Answer 65**

To drum up support for The Clean Air Act, the first Earth Day was organized on April 22, 1970, by Wisconsin Senator Gaylord Nelson. Nelson received help from a Harvard graduate named Denis Hayes, who organized a global Earth Day event in 1990. The holiday is now one of the United Nations' official international holidays.

# The Best Facts
# For Smart Kids

**Question 66**

In what Tennessee city is the Jack Daniel's distillery located?

a) Memphis

b) Lynchburg

c) Chattanooga

d) Knoxville

**Answer 66**

The Jack Daniel's distillery is in Lynchburg, Tennessee. Ironically, Jack Daniels whiskey is not for sale in Lynchburg because the city is in a dry county, meaning liquor cannot be sold there. However, the distillery does sell commemorative bottles that just happen to be filled with Jack Daniels' Tennessee whiskey.

# The Best Facts
# For Smart Kids

**Question 67**

What celestial object is also the name of one of Santa's reindeer?

a) Pluto

b) Comet

c) Cupid

d) Donner

**Answer 67**

Comets are frozen snowballs of gas and rock left over from the creation of the Solar System. When comets enter the sun's orbit, the heat causes it to spew gas and dust in a spectacular display that can be seen in the night sky.

# The Best Facts
# For Smart Kids

**Question 68**

In which current country is the old capital of the Inca Empire, Cuzco, located?

a) Peru

b) Brazil

c) Mexico

d) Argentina

**Answer 68**

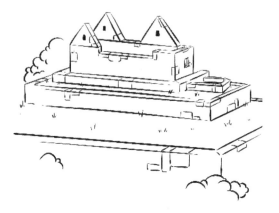

The City of Cuzco is located in South America, in present-day Peru. It was the capital of the Inca Empire. It was built about six hundred years ago and was over ten thousand feet above sea level in the Peruvian Andes. It was destined for religious ceremonies and administrative activities.

# The Best Facts
# For Smart Kids

**Question 69**

What year was the word Friendsgiving added to the Merriam-Webster dictionary?

a) 2020

b) 1999

c) 2007

d) 1992

# David W. Leon
## Fun Facts Books

**Answer 69**

After being on the dictionary's "Words We're Watching," Friendsgiving became an official word in 2020, although it is not yet an official holiday. Most people host Friendsgiving on Thanksgiving (if they can't be with family) or choose to have it sometime before the family Thanksgiving dinner.

# The Best Facts
# For Smart Kids

**Question 70**

What is the name of the Roman amphitheater ("theater in the round") that once hosted gladiator battles?

a) Red Rocks

b) The Colosseum

c) Dalhalla

d) Slane Castle

**Answer 70**

Built of stone and concrete by slaves, the Colosseum in Roma, Italy, is 189m long, 156m wide, and 50m high. The games at the Colosseum were free, and the building could seat up to 50,000 people who entered through 80 entrances. While most of the Colosseum has been destroyed by natural disasters and vandalism, it is a popular tourist destination.

# The Best Facts
# For Smart Kids

## Question 71

Which is the weakest force in nature?

a)  The weak force

b)  Gravity

c)  Electromagnetic force

d)  Strong force

**Answer 71**

Compared to the other fundamental forces in nature - the strong nuclear force, the electromagnetic force, and the weak nuclear force - gravity is significantly weaker. Gravitational force is the attractive force between objects with mass. It acts over long distances and is responsible for the interaction between celestial bodies like planets, stars, and galaxies.

# The Best Facts
# For Smart Kids

**Question 72**

Which Native American civilization built Machu Picchu in the middle of the Andes Mountains?

a) The Peruvians

b) The Mayans

c) The Bush people

d) The Incas

**Answer 72**

Machu Picchu was built by the Incas in Peru at 7,970 feet above sea level on the Andes. They developed a complex agricultural system to leverage the slopes (Jarus, 2012). Besides, they were able to construct their houses and other structures with heavy rocks they moved even without the benefit of wheels.

# The Best Facts
# For Smart Kids

## Question 73

What is another name for the Tibetan New Year?

a) Palden Lhamo Festival

b) Losar Festival

c) Chokhor Duchen Festival

d) Saga Dawa Festival

**Answer 73**

Both the most traditional festival of the Tibetan calendar and the first festival of the year, the Losar Festival is based on two Tibetan words: "Lo" means year, and "Sar" means new. The festival lasts for fifteen days and is the time to pray for good crops in the coming year. In addition to dancing and singing, Tibetans also chant Buddhist scriptures, dress in traditional costumes, and pass torches in the street to dispel any evil while also praying for good luck.

# The Best Facts
# For Smart Kids

**Question 74**

What famous island prison's name means "pelican?"

a)  Alcatraz

b)  Devil's Island

c)  Sing Sing

d)  Port Arthur

# David W. Leon
# Fun Facts Books

**Answer 74**

The island of Alcatraz was originally called "La Isla de los Alcatraces," meaning "Island of the Pelicans" because of the hundreds of pelicans that resided there. The small island in San Francisco Bay was also the location of the first lighthouse on the west coast before the maximum security prison was built. The prison closed in 1963 because it was too expensive to operate, but has now become a popular tourist destination.

# The Best Facts
# For Smart Kids

**Question 75**

Which type of cloud produces the highest amount of hail due to its strong updrafts?

a)  Cumulonimbus

b)  Altocumulus

c)  Stratus

d)  Cirrus

**Answer 75**

Cumulonimbus clouds often develop in association with thunderstorms and can reach great heights in the atmosphere. The presence of strong updrafts within these clouds allows hailstones to remain suspended in the cloud, accumulating layers of ice until they become too heavy and fall to the ground.

# The Best Facts
# For Smart Kids

## Question 76

What are the moai?

a) Giant human statues

b) Small stone pyramids

c) Animal figures like the Sphinx

d) Lines drawn in the stone

# David W. Leon
# Fun Facts Books

**Answer 76**

The moai are giant, stone-made human figures which are half-buried in the ground. Only the heads are visible, and the rest of the bodies are covered. There are about a thousand 32-feet-tall statues carved on a single piece of stone with a tool called toki.

# The Best Facts
# For Smart Kids

**Question 77**

What month-long festival is considered the holiest of the Tibetan calendar?

a) Saga Dawa Festival

b) Palden Lhamo Festival

c) Bathing Festival

d) Nagqu Horse Racing Festival

**Answer 77**

Also known as the "Festival for Releasing Living Things," the Saga Dawa Festival focuses on paying homage to Buddha and the Buddhist desire to lead a noble life. During this festival, Tibetans make pilgrimages to sacred sites, give money to beggars, and light lamps known as "butter lamps" because of the clarified yak butter used as oil.

# The Best Facts
# For Smart Kids

**Question 78**

The Leshan Buddha, the world's largest Buddha statue, is in what country?

a) Korea

b) Vietnam

c) India

d) China

# David W. Leon
# Fun Facts Books

**Answer 78**

The world's largest stone Buddha statue was carved into the hillside of the Xiguo Peak, a mountain located in Sichuan province of China. This 233-foot-tall Buddha has a drainage system built behind the statue's head and ears that has prevented erosion from damaging the enormous statue for over 1200 years.

# The Best Facts
# For Smart Kids

**Question 79**

What is it called when you feel like you've experienced something before, even though you know that you haven't?

a) Déjà vu

b) Folie à deux

c) L'agnosie

d) Amok

**Answer 79**

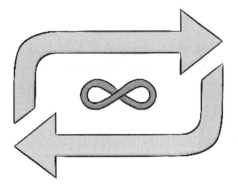

Déjà vu refers to the feeling or sensation of having already experienced a current situation, even though it is objectively impossible. In French, the term means "already seen," and may be linked to memory processing and retrieval. It's possible that people who have better memory recall or stronger memory associations may experience déjà vu more often.

# The Best Facts
# For Smart Kids

**Question 80**

Why did Christopher Columbus venture across the Atlantic Ocean?

a) Spain wanted to conquer America

b) Spain needed new trading routes

c) England wanted new places to trade with

d) Ottoman Empire sent Columbus on a mission

**Answer 80**

Christopher Columbus searched for new navigation routes to replace the Mediterranean Sea, occupied by the Ottomans in the 15th century. The Spanish Catholic monarchs funded the expedition, as they needed a new path to continue to trade with southeast Asia. Columbus made his first journey with a crew of convicts.

# Level 5
## Discover The Unknown

## Questions 81-100

We've Covered Science, History, Holidays, And Traveled The World. I Hope You've Discovered Some New Things To Learn About Further!

# The Best Facts
# For Smart Kids

**Question 81**

What is the most popular food at the Tibetan Shoton Festival?

a) Zanba

b) Yogurt

c) Noodles

d) Mog Rice

# David W. Leon
# Fun Facts Books

**Answer 81**

The word Shoton is a combination of two Tibetan words, - "sho" which means yogurt and "ton" means banquet - so the name of the festival literally translates to "Festival of Eating Yogurt." In addition to the yogurt, families celebrate by having picnics including butter tea, or Qingke liquor.

# The Best Facts
# For Smart Kids

**Question 82**

Overlooking Los Angeles, what did the iconic Hollywood sign use to say before it was restored and changed in 1949?

a) Angel Town

b) La-La Land

c) Hollywoodland

d) Tinseltown

# David W. Leon
## Fun Facts Books

**Answer 82**

In 1923, Los Angeles Times publisher Harry Chandler planned to build an upscale neighborhood called "Hollywoodland," but the Great Depression ruined his real estate dreams. After years of neglect, the Hollywood Chamber of Commerce took over care of the sign, including having the last four letters removed so that the sign simply read "Hollywood".

# The Best Facts
# For Smart Kids

**Question 83**

What planet is also known as "Morning Star?"

a) Mercury

b) Pluto

c) Venus

d) Mars

**Answer 83**

Despite being a planet, Venus is often called "Morning Star" or "Evening Star," depending on when it becomes visible in the sky. Unlike other planets, Venus is always close to the sun. Depending on which side of the sun it is orbiting, it will be one of the first objects to appear in the morning or night sky.

# The Best Facts
# For Smart Kids

**Question 84**

Which of the following wasn't one of the thirteen colonies before the United States became independent?

a)  Massachusetts

b)  Rhode Island

c)  Maryland

d)  Louisiana

**Answer 84**

The thirteen colonies were the former English settlements on the northeast coast of North America. Louisiana wasn't one of those initial settlements. Instead, it was an extensive territory in the Mississippi river basin between the Appalachian and the Rocky Mountains.

# The Best Facts
# For Smart Kids

**Question 85**

What is the public holiday in Fiji that marks the day that indentured servants from India arrived on the island?

a)  Fiji Day

b)  Girmit Day

c)  Constitution Day

d)  Boxing Day

**Answer 85**

Marked as a day of remembrance for Indian indentured servants who were brought to the island in 1897 to work on sugar cane plantations, Girmit Day is named after girmit, the Indian word for agreement. It is celebrated on May 14th or May 15th annually and is usually marked by speeches and parades.

# The Best Facts
# For Smart Kids

**Question 86**

In what South American country will you *not* find the Amazon rainforest?

a)  Chile

b)  Brazil

c)  Columbia

d)  Ecuador

**Answer 86**

The Amazon rainforest spreads throughout nine countries: Brazil, Colombia, Peru, Venezuela, Ecuador, Bolivia, and the three Guianas. Much of the rainforest is found in Brazil where the Manaus (2m people) and Belém (1.4m people) live.

# The Best Facts
# For Smart Kids

**Question 87**

From which body part does most of your body heat escape?

a) Head

b) Feet

c) Nose

d) It escapes evenly

# David W. Leon
# Fun Facts Books

**Answer 87**

Despite what your mother may have told you, you will only lose ten percent of your body heat through your head without a hat. Heat escapes the body evenly through the skin. How much heat you lose depends on how much skin you have exposed to the cold.

# The Best Facts
# For Smart Kids

**Question 88**

Which European country sold Louisiana to the United States?

a)  Spain

b)  England

c)  France

d)  Italy

**Answer 88**

Louisiana used to belong to Spain. In 1802, Napoleon Bonaparte invaded Spain and its territories in America became French. This was considered a threat by the US government but after a diplomatic intervention, Bonaparte decided to sell Louisiana to the United States for $15,000,000.

## Question 89

What is Valentine's Day called in Romania?

a) Brâncu□i Day

b) Măr□i□orul

c) Dragobete

d) Rusaliile

**Answer 89**

In Romania, February 24th marks not only the unofficial beginning of spring, but a yearly celebration of love called Dragobete. Dragobete is a figure in Romanian mythology who is seen as a protector of lovers and birds. Dragobete is considered the perfect time to express your romantic interest in someone.

**Question 90**

What limestone structure has a name that means "high city" in Greek?

a)  Corinthian Capital

b)  Erechtheion

c)  Stoa of Attalos

d)  Acropolis

**Answer 90**

Built on a plateau overlooking the city of Athens, the Acropolis is one of Greece's most architectural triumphs. Its construction began during the Bronze Age, and during its heyday, from 460 B.C. to 430 B.C, the Acropolis was composed of several Greek temples. The Acropolis was likely destroyed or repurposed into Christian churches after the Romans occupied the country and converted to Christianity.

# The Best Facts
# For Smart Kids

**Question 91**

Which famous chess-playing computer defeated world chess champion Garry Kasparov in 1997?

a) Hal 9000

b) Siri

c) Deep Blue

d) Cerebex

**Answer 91**

Developed by IBM, Deep Blue became the first computer to defeat a reigning world chess champion in a six-game match. It was a significant milestone in the development of artificial intelligence and machine learning in the field of chess. Deep Blue defeated Kasparov in only thirty-seven chess moves, and its designer said the computer was able to analyze 100,000 chess moves per second.

# The Best Facts
# For Smart Kids

**Question 92**

When did humans land on the moon?

a)   1920

b)   1997

c)   2019

d)   1969

**Answer 92**

The first spaceship to accomplish the objective of "landing" on the moon's surface happened on July 20, 1969. The NASA mission had a crew made up of three astronauts from the US. After doing the first moon walk in history, the crew was able to return safely to Earth four days later.

# The Best Facts
# For Smart Kids

**Question 93**

What country celebrates a "love day" on the 14th of every month?

a) Japan

b) Iceland

c) Korea

d) Sweden

**Answer 93**

In addition to celebrating Valentine's Day on February 14th, Korea celebrates a romantic holiday each month, including Diary Day (January), White Day (March), Black Day (April), Rose Day (May), Kiss Day (June), Silver Day (July), Green Day (August), Photo Day (September), Wine Day (October), Movie Day (November), and Hug Day (December). Two of the most popular dates are March's White Day, when men give their significant lovers something white, and April's Black Day, when single people who did not receive a Valentine's Day gift gather and eat black noodles.

# The Best Facts
# For Smart Kids

**Question 94**

What dam in Nevada was once the Earth's tallest dam?

a) Hoover Dam

b) Three Gorges Dam

c) Glen Canyon Dam

d) Oahe Dam

# David W. Leon
# Fun Facts Books

**Answer 94**

When built in the 1930s, the Hoover Dam was 726.4 feet tall, making it the tallest dam in the world. However, in 1968, the Oroville Dam in California surpassed the Hoover Dam at 770 feet. In 2013, the Jinping-I Dam, the world's tallest dam, became operational in China.

# The Best Facts
# For Smart Kids

**Question 95**

How long did dinosaurs dominate the Earth?

a)  165 million years

b)  2 million years

c)  5 years

d)  100 years

**Answer 95**

Dinosaurs first appeared during the Mesozoic Era, specifically in the late Triassic period, approximately 230 million years ago. They remained the dominant land-dwelling creatures for about 165 million years, until their extinction at the end of the Cretaceous period, around 65.5 million years ago. For perspective, humans have only been around for two million years.

# The Best Facts
# For Smart Kids

**Question 96**

What were the Roman emperors called as a sign of respect?

a) Pharaoh

b) Your Honour

c) Your Kindness

d) Caesar Augustus

**Answer 96**

Romans gave their emperors the title of Caesar Augustus to honor Julius Caesar. His heir, Octavian, was the first emperor of the Roman Empire after Julius Caesar was assassinated by a conspiracy. He was named after his father and took the name of all the future emperors of the dynasty.

# The Best Facts
# For Smart Kids

**Question 97**

What festival of lights marks the beginning of Christmas in Scandinavian countries?

a) St. Lucia's Day

b) Shrove Tuesday

c) Saint John's Eve

d) Walpurgis Night

**Answer 97**

In Norway, it's called Lussinatten, in Denmark, the name is Luciadag, and in Sweden, the practice is called Lucia, or Saint Lucy's Day. Saint Lucy is believed to be a carrier of light during the dark Scandinavian winters and is honored by people wearing white gowns and carrying candles. In Norway and Sweden, the holiday is considered a secular holiday, but in Denmark it is considered a religious holiday.

# The Best Facts
# For Smart Kids

**Question 98**

Which island is the home of some of the biggest tortoises in the world?

a) Cuba

b) The Galapagos Islands

c) Greenland

d) Dominica

**Answer 98**

Named after the Spanish word for tortoise, the Galapagos Islands are home to twelve species of turtles that can grow up to five feet and weigh over 500 pounds. The Galapagos Islands are considered part of Ecuador because they're located 563 miles off Ecuador's coast.

# The Best Facts
# For Smart Kids

**Question 99**

Sharing its name with the son of Poseidon, what is the name of the moon that orbits Neptune backwards?

a) Triton

b) Jupiter

c) Aether

d) Apollo

# David W. Leon
# Fun Facts Books

**Answer 99**

Discovered in 1846, Triton is an unusual moon that moves retrograde around Neptune. Triton is the largest of Neptune's thirteen moons and is one of the coldest places in our solar system.

# The Best Facts
# For Smart Kids

**Question 100**

What type of paper did the Egyptians use to write on in hieroglyphics?

a) Quipus

b) Papyrus

c) Carbon tissue

d) Stone paper

**Answer 100**

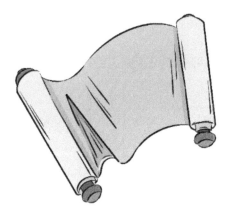

Apart from carving hieroglyphics on stone, Egyptians developed a type of paper: papyrus. It was made from a plant that grew on the banks of the Nile River. They took the internal layer of the plant's stalk and pressed it. The strips of papyrus were used for legal and religious texts.

# Thank You & Leave A Review

Have you ever tried something scary and new, and it seems the odds are against you? If yes, then you likely know exactly how my wife and I feel right now.

We're taking a leap and trying our hand at writing and sharing our favorite family tradition of trivia night.

Our goal is to create high quality books for everyone to enjoy and hopefully learn a few new things too.

Your feedback will help us to keep writing these books and it would mean a lot to hear from you.

Posting a review is the best and easiest way to support the work of independent authors like us. If you've enjoyed any of our books so far and have 2 minutes to spare, we would be so thankful!

We truly appreciate all your love and support!

Open the camera app on your phone
Hold phone so the QR Code appears in view
Tap the pop-up link for the QR Code

# Your Free Gift

Grab your FREE Gifts:

**BONUS 1**: Our best-selling e-book

**BONUS 2**: An exclusive, never-before-seen, e-book with an additional 100 interesting and fun facts!

Open the camera app on your phone
Hold phone so the QR Code appears in view
Tap the pop-up link for the QR Code

# Check Out The Full Series

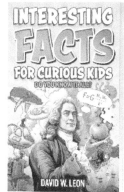  

Enjoyed the book?
Check out the full series!

Open the camera app on your phone
Hold phone so the QR Code appears in view
Tap the pop-up link for the QR Code